THABISO PENYENYE

The Terror Of This World

A journey Through Environmental collapse, Isolation and the shadows of our time

Contents

Introduction

In the quiet moments before dawn, when the world is still and darkness clings to the horizon, there lies a terror that is both ancient and ever-present. It is the fear that resides in the hearts of those who have seen the worst of humanity, the dread that follows in the wake of disaster, and the anxiety that lingers in the shadows of our minds. This terror takes many forms—war, poverty, oppression, environmental collapse, disease, and isolation—and it has shaped the course of human history in profound and often tragic ways.

The terror of this world is not confined to the pages of history books or the distant lands we see on the news. It is a part of our daily lives, woven into the fabric of our existence. It is the mother who fears for her child's future in a war-torn country, the family struggling to make ends meet in the face of economic despair, the activist who risks everything to speak out against injustice, and the individual who battles the silent torment of mental illness.

Yet, in the face of such overwhelming terror, there is also hope. Hope that, despite the darkness, humanity has the capacity for compassion, resilience, and change. Hope that, by confronting the terrors of this world, we can forge a path toward a better future.

This book is a journey through the many faces of terror that haunt our world. It is an exploration of the fear that grips us, the pain that endures, and the courage that arises in the most desperate of times. Through stories, analysis, and reflection, we will delve into the terror of this world, not to be consumed by it, but to understand it, confront it, and ultimately, find a way to overcome it.

Chapter 1: The Terror of War

The Legacy Of Conflict

War is as old as humanity itself. From the earliest tribal skirmishes to the massive global conflicts of the 20th century, the history of war is a history of terror. Each battle, each campaign, has brought with it a unique kind of fear—one that is born from the knowledge that life can be snuffed out in an instant.

But the terror of war does not end when the fighting stops. The survivors— those who manage to escape the clutches of death— carry with them the weight of what they have seen and done. The memories of war, etched into their minds, often return to haunt them long after the guns have fallen silent. For many, the battlefield is never truly left behind.

Think about Anna, a nurse who worked in the trenches during World War I. She saw terrible things that most people could not imagine—limbs torn apart by explosions, men screaming in pain as they bled in the mud, and the eyes of dying soldiers looking at her, asking for help she couldn't give. Even decades later, she still had nightmares. She would wake up in the middle of the night, soaked in sweat, with the sounds of war in her ears. The fear from those days had become a part of her, like a ghost that wouldn't go away.

The Civilians' Nightmare

War does not only terrorize those who fight—it also wreaks havoc on the lives of those who are caught in its crossfire. For civilians, the terror of war is often a daily reality, one that involves constant fear for their lives and the lives of their loved ones.

Take the story of Abdul, a young boy living in Aleppo during the Syrian Civil War. He grew up in a city where the sound of explosions was more common than the sound of laughter. His home was destroyed in an airstrike, his school reduced to rubble, and his family scattered. Each day was a battle for survival— finding food, water, and shelter in a city that had been torn apart. The terror that Abdul experienced was not just the fear of death, but the fear of a life that had been shattered beyond repair.

The terror of war extends beyond the immediate physical dangers. It is also the psychological torment of living in a world where nothing is certain,
where the rules of civilization have been suspended, and where the future is a dark, impenetrable void.

The Generational Impact

T

he terror of war is not confined to the battlefield or the immediate aftermath. It reverberates through generations, affecting the children and grandchildren of those who lived through it. The trauma of war can be passed down, manifesting in ways that are not always obvious but are deeply felt.

In post-war societies, the scars of conflict can be seen in the eyes of those who have inherited the memories of terror. These societies often grapple with a collective trauma, one that shapes their national identity and influences their actions on the global stage. The fear of another conflict, of history repeating itself, lingers in the background, shaping policies and perceptions.

Stories of Resilience

Y

et, amid the terror of war, there are also stories of resilience—of individuals and communities who, despite the horrors they faced, found a way to survive, to rebuild, and to move forward. These stories are a testament to the strength of the human spirit, to the capacity for hope even in the darkest of times.

One such story is that of Hiroshi, a survivor of the atomic bombing of Hiroshima. He lost everything in the blast—his family, his home, his city. But he refused to give in to despair. He dedicated his life to advocating for peace, to ensuring that the terror of nuclear war would never be repeated. His story is one of many that show that even in the face of unimaginable terror, there is the possibility of redemption and renewal.

The Wounds That Never Heal

W

ar leaves behind physical destruction that is often visible—destroyed cities, shattered infrastructure, scorched landscapes—but the deepest wounds are the ones that are not seen, those that
are carried within the human heart and mind. These invisible scars can take years, even generations, to heal, if they ever heal at all.

For veterans, the return to civilian life is often fraught with difficulty. The transition from the chaos of the battlefield to the relative peace of home can be jarring. Many soldiers find themselves haunted by memories of what they've seen and done. The psychological trauma—what we now recognize as Post-Traumatic Stress Disorder (PTSD)—can be debilitating. Flashbacks, nightmares, anxiety, and depression become constant companions, turning the peace they fought so hard to achieve into a personal hell.

The Story of John

John, a veteran of the Vietnam War, is one such example. He was just 19 when he was drafted, a boy from a small town in the Midwest, thrust into a conflict he neither understood nor supported. The jungles of Vietnam were a world away from the quiet streets he had known, a world where death lurked behind every tree, where the enemy was often invisible but always present.

John survived the war, but the war never left him. For years after his return, he struggled to find his place in a world that had moved on without him. The sound of helicopters would send him spiraling back to the jungles, the smell of burning wood would trigger memories of napalm strikes. He couldn't sleep without nightmares, and when he did sleep, it was fitful, restless.

He tried to bury his experiences, to forget the faces of the friends he lost, to push away the guilt he felt for surviving when so many did not. But the memories refused to be silenced. He turned to alcohol to numb the pain, but it only made things worse. His marriage fell apart, his relationship with his children strained under the weight of the unspoken horrors he carried with him.

It was only years later, after seeking help from a veterans' support group, that John began to confront his past. Sharing his story with others who understood his pain was the first step toward healing. But the scars remained, a reminder of the terror he endured, a terror that would always be a part of him.

The Ripple Effects on Society

The terror of war extends far beyond the battlefield. The societies left behind in its wake often face decades of turmoil. The economic, political, and social structures that are torn apart by conflict can take generations to rebuild, if they ever fully recover.

T

he Case of Post-War Bosnia

Consider Bosnia, a country that endured a brutal civil war in the 1990s. The war, marked by ethnic cleansing and mass atrocities, left deep scars on the nation. The physical destruction was immense— entire towns were razed to the ground, infrastructure was obliterated, and landmines littered the countryside. But the psychological scars ran even deeper.

In the years following the war, Bosnia struggled to rebuild. The economy was in shambles, with unemployment rates soaring and poverty widespread. But perhaps the most significant impact was on the social fabric of the country. The war had pitted neighbor against neighbor, friend against friend, and those divisions did not simply disappear when the fighting stopped.

The trauma of the war manifested in various ways—high rates of mental illness, domestic violence, and substance abuse. The youth, many of whom had no memory of the war itself, grew up in a society marked by mistrust and fear. The wounds of the past were passed down to the next generation, creating a cycle of trauma that continues to affect the country today.

Efforts to heal these wounds have been ongoing, with peace-building initiatives, truth and reconciliation commissions, and mental health programs. But the road to recovery is long, and the terror of the past still lingers in the collective consciousness of the nation.

The Fear of What Comes Next

O

ne of the most insidious aspects of the terror of war is the fear of what comes next. For those who live in conflict zones, even when a war ends, there is often no guarantee that peace will follow. The fear that violence could erupt again at any moment keeps communities on edge, preventing them from fully moving forward.

L

iving in a Perpetual State of Fear

In places like Afghanistan, where decades of conflict have created a cycle of violence, this fear is a daily reality. Even in times of relative peace, the threat of violence hangs over the population like a dark cloud. Bombings, assassinations, and other acts of terror continue to disrupt daily life, making it impossible for people to feel safe, even in their own homes.

This constant state of fear takes a toll on mental health, leading to widespread anxiety, depression, and other psychological issues. Children grow up in a world where violence is normalized, where the sound of explosions is just another part of the day. The long-term impact of living in such an environment is profound, affecting everything from education and employment to family relationships and social cohesion.

The Global Implications

T

he terror of war is not confined to the countries where the fighting takes place. In our interconnected world, the consequences of conflict can ripple outwards, affecting global stability and security.

The Refugee Crisis

One of the most visible impacts of war is the refugee crisis. Millions of people are forced to flee their homes in search of safety, creating humanitarian emergencies in neighboring countries and beyond. The influx of refugees can strain resources, create political tensions, and even lead to further conflict in the regions that host them.

The plight of refugees is a stark reminder of the human cost of war. These are people who have lost everything—their homes, their livelihoods, their sense of security. They often face uncertain futures, trapped in limbo, unable to return home but also unable to fully integrate into their new surroundings.

International Responses

The global response to war is often mixed. While some conflicts draw widespread attention and intervention, others are ignored or forgotten. The reasons for this disparity are complex, involving geopolitical interests, media coverage, and public perception. But the result is the same—countless lives are lost or destroyed while the world looks on, often doing too little, too late.

Efforts to stop war and reduce its effects are ongoing, with international organizations, governments, and NGOs working to promote peace, give aid, and rebuild societies damaged by war. However, the challenges are huge, and the path to peace is full of difficulties.

Conclusion: The Unending Battle

T

he terror of war is a force that has shaped the course of history, leaving in its wake a legacy of destruction, trauma, and fear. It is a terror that transcends borders, affecting individuals and societies in profound and lasting ways.

Yet, even in the face of this terror, there is hope. The stories of those who have survived, who have rebuilt their lives and their communities, remind us that the human spirit is resilient. The efforts of those who work tirelessly to prevent war, to heal its wounds, and to promote peace are a testament to the possibility of a better future. But the battle is far from over. As long as there are conflicts in the world, the terror of war will continue to haunt us. It is up to us, as a global community, to confront this terror, to work towards peace, and to ensure that future generations do not have to endure the same horrors.

Chapter 2: The Terror of Poverty

The Daily Struggle for Survival

I

n the crowded undeveloped streets of Yizo-yizo, North West, life is a constant struggle against deep poverty. Narrow paths wind through homes made from bits of wood, metal, and plastic. The air is filled with the smell of sewage, and the sounds of children crying, and the noise of daily life blend into a chaotic mix.

For those living there, every day is a struggle for survival. Basic necessities— food, clean water, shelter—are luxuries that are not always guaranteed. In the face of this uncertainty, fear becomes a constant companion. The terror of poverty is not just about hunger or homelessness; it is the all-encompassing dread that tomorrow might be worse than today, that the fragile threads holding life together could snap at any moment.

A

Mother's Fear

Consider the story of Lizzy, a mother of three who lives in Yizoyizo. Every morning, she wakes up before dawn to collect water
from a communal tap, hoping to get enough before the lines grow too long. She works as a maid in a wealthy household, earning barely enough to feed her children one meal a day. Her husband, unemployed, often comes home late, exhausted and empty-handed after a long day of gambling and drinking.

Lizzy's greatest fear is not her own hunger or exhaustion; it is the fear that her children will go to bed with empty stomachs, that they will fall ill from the contaminated water, or that they will be forced to drop out of school because she cannot afford the fees and school uniform. This fear gnaws at her constantly, a relentless reminder of the precariousness of her existence.

The terror of poverty is the fear of not knowing if you will have enough to survive, the anxiety of being one illness, one accident, or one bad day away from losing everything. It is a fear that drains hope, saps energy, and makes every decision a matter of life and death.

The Inescapable Trap

P
overty is not just a temporary state; for many, it is a trap from which escape seems impossible. This sense of entrapment, of

being stuck in a cycle that offers no way out, adds another layer of terror to the already overwhelming daily struggles.

24

T

he Cycle of Poverty

In many parts of the world, poverty is passed down from one generation to the next, creating a cycle that is difficult to break. Lack of access to education, healthcare, and economic opportunities means that children born into poverty are likely to remain in poverty as adults. This cycle perpetuates inequality and leaves entire communities trapped in a perpetual state of fear and deprivation.

Take the story of John, a young boy growing up in a rural village in Limpopo. His family, like many others in the village, relies on subsistence farming to survive. The land they farm is poor, and the yields are often barely enough to feed them. There is no money for school, and John spends his days helping his father in the fields instead of learning in a classroom.

John dreams of a different life, of escaping the village and finding a job in the city. But without education or skills, his prospects are bleak. The opportunities that could lift him out of poverty are out of reach, and he knows that he will likely follow in his father's footsteps, trapped in the same cycle of poverty that has defined his family's existence for generations.

The terror of poverty is not just the fear of today's hardships; it is the fear that tomorrow will bring more of the same, that the future holds no promise of relief or improvement. It is the dread of seeing one's children inherit the same struggles and knowing that there is little you can do to change their fate.

The Hidden Costs of Poverty

P

overty is often linked with things we can see, like worn-out clothes, broken-down homes, and poor nutrition. But its effects go much deeper. The hidden costs of poverty are psychological, social, and
emotional, and they can be just as harmful as the physical hardships.

The Psychological Toll

Living in poverty takes a heavy toll on mental health. The constant stress of trying to make ends meet, the shame and stigma associated
with poverty, and the feeling of helplessness can lead to anxiety, depression, and other mental health issues. The fear of poverty becomes internalized, creating a sense of worthlessness and despair.

Maria's Struggle

Maria, a single mother living outside of Rustenburg, South Africa, knows this all too well. After losing her job at a factory that closed down, she has been unable to find stable employment. Her days are spent searching for work, any work, to provide for her two young children. But jobs are scarce, and the few she finds are poorly paid and short-term.

Maria's fear is not just about providing for her children; it is the fear that she is failing them, that her inability to escape poverty is a reflection of her own inadequacy. This fear has begun to erode her self-esteem, leaving her feeling isolated and hopeless. The terror of poverty is not just the external challenges; it is the internal battle against the belief that you are less valuable, less capable, less deserving because of your circumstances.

T

he Social Isolation

Poverty also leads to social isolation. The lack of resources and opportunities often pushes people to the margins of society, where they are excluded from the networks and communities that could offer support. This isolation exacerbates the terror of poverty, as individuals and families are left to face their struggles alone, without the social safety nets that might provide some relief.

In many places, poverty is stigmatized, leading to discrimination and exclusion. The poor are often blamed for their situation, seen as lazy or irresponsible, rather than victims of systemic inequality and injustice. This blame adds to the terror, creating a sense of shame that prevents people from seeking help or speaking out about their struggles

.

Breaking the

cycle

D

espite the overwhelming challenges, there are stories of individuals and communities who have managed to break free from the cycle of poverty. These stories offer a glimmer of hope, showing that with the right support, it is possible to overcome the terror of poverty.

Empowerment Through Education

Education is often seen as the key to breaking the cycle of poverty. In places where access to education has been improved, the impact on poverty reduction has been significant. Programs that provide scholarships, build schools, and support teachers have lifted entire communities out of poverty, giving children the tools they need to create a better future.

Malala's Legacy

The story of Malala Yousafzai, a Pakistani girl who defied the Taliban to fight for her right to education, is a powerful example of how education can be a force for change. Malala's courage in the face of terror—both the terror of the Taliban and the terror of poverty—has inspired millions around the world. Her advocacy for girls' education has brought attention to the importance of education in breaking the cycle of poverty and empowering the next generation.

Community-Led Solutions

In many parts of the world, communities have come together to find solutions to poverty that are tailored to their specific needs. Microfinance initiatives, cooperative businesses, and local development projects have provided people with the resources and support they need to improve their lives. These grassroots efforts have shown that, with the right tools and a sense of solidarity, it is possible to confront the terror of poverty and build a better future.

Conclusion: The Fight Against Poverty

The fear of poverty is strong and affects millions of people around the world. It comes from daily struggles, the feeling of being stuck in a cycle with no escape, and the deep inequalities within and between
societies. But it is not a fear that we can't overcome.

The fight against poverty is ongoing, and while the challenges are immense, there are also signs of progress. Education, empowerment, and community led solutions are key to breaking the cycle of poverty and providing people with the opportunities they need to improve their lives. The stories of those who have overcome poverty, who have found ways to break free from its grip, offer hope that it is possible to confront and conquer this terror.

As a global community, we must continue to address the root causes of poverty, to provide support and resources to those in need, and to work towards a world where everyone has the opportunity to live a life free from the fear of poverty.

Chapter 3: The Terror of Oppression

O

ppression is a silent, pervasive form of terror that grinds down the human spirit. Unlike the immediate destruction of war or disease, oppression inflicts a slow, relentless suffering on its victims, stripping away their rights, freedoms, and dignity. It is a terror that often operates in the shadows, where fear is used as a tool to control, manipulate, and suppress.

North Korea: A Nation Enslaved

North Korea, one of the most repressive regimes in the world, is a chilling example of how a government can use terror to maintain absolute control over its people. Under the rule of the Kim dynasty, the North Korean state has built a system of extreme surveillance, censorship, and punishment, where even the smallest act of dissent can lead to imprisonment, torture, or execution.

The fear in North Korea is omnipresent. Citizens are required to show absolute loyalty to the regime, with public displays of devotion to the leader, Kim Jong-un, being mandatory. Any deviation from this can result in severe
punishment, not just for the individual but for their entire family. The concept of "guilt by association" means that families can be punished for the actions of one member, creating a culture of fear and mistrust.

The terror of living under such a regime extends beyond the physical punishments. The constant surveillance, the enforced isolation from the outside world, and the relentless propaganda create a psychological prison where fear is internalized. For many North Koreans, the terror is in the knowledge that there is no escape, no possibility of freedom or a better life.

The Crushing Weight of Discrimination

O

ppression is not always enforced by a single ruler or government; it can also take the form of systemic discrimination, where entire groups of people are marginalized, silenced, and denied their basic human rights.

A

partheid in South Africa: The Rule of Fear

The apartheid era in South Africa, which lasted from 1948 to 1994, was a time of institutionalized racial oppression that systematically dehumanized the country's non-white population. Under apartheid, black South Africans were subjected to a brutal regime that segregated every aspect of life—where they could live, work, and even walk. The laws were enforced with ruthless efficiency, and any attempt to resist or protest was met with violent repression.

For black South Africans, the terror of apartheid was not just in the physical violence inflicted by the state but in the daily humiliations and degradations that were part of life under the system. The constant fear of arrest, beatings, or worse, for simply being in the wrong place at the wrong time, was a reality for millions. The psychological impact of living under such a system— where your very existence was deemed inferior—left deep scars on the nation's psyche.

The end of apartheid did not immediately erase the terror it inflicted. The legacy of fear, mistrust, and division continued to shape South African society long after the official end of the regime. The transition to a new, democratic South Africa required not just legal and political changes, but a process of healing and reconciliation to address the deep wounds left by decades of oppression.

The Terror of Genocide

G

enocide represents the most extreme form of oppression, where the intent is not just to subjugate, but to eliminate an entire group of people. The terror of genocide is the fear of total annihilation, driven by hatred, ideology, or the desire for power.

The Holocaust: The Abyss of Human Cruelty

The Holocaust, orchestrated by Nazi Germany during World War II, stands as one of the darkest chapters in human history. Over six million Jews, along with millions of others including Romani people, disabled individuals, and political dissidents, were systematically exterminated in concentration camps and killing fields across Europe.

The terror of the Holocaust was multifaceted. For the victims, the fear began with the rise of anti-Semitic laws and propaganda, which slowly stripped them of their rights, property, and dignity. As the Nazi regime's genocidal intent became clear, the fear of being discovered, rounded up, and deported to a camp became a daily reality. In the camps, the terror reached its peak, as people were subjected to unimaginable cruelty, forced labor, starvation, and the constant threat of death.

The Holocaust was not just a crime of murder; it was a crime of dehumanization. The Nazi regime's efforts to portray Jews and other targeted groups as subhuman, deserving of extermination, were part of the terror. The systematic nature of the genocide, with its industrial-scale killing machinery, represented a terrifying new form of oppression, where the power of the state was harnessed to eradicate entire populations.

The aftermath of the Holocaust left survivors with profound psychological
trauma, haunted by the memories of what they endured and the loss of their loved ones. The terror of genocide is a collective experience, one that leaves a lasting impact on the identity and history of the people who suffer it.

The Struggle for Freedom

O

ppression breeds resistance, and throughout history, the oppressed have fought back against their oppressors, often at great personal risk. The struggle for freedom is a powerful antidote to the terror of oppression, but it is a struggle that is often fraught with danger.

T

he Civil Rights Movement: Confronting Injustice

The Civil Rights Movement in the United States during the 1950s and 1960s was a pivotal moment in the fight against racial oppression. Led by figures such as Martin Luther King Jr., Rosa Parks, and many others, the movement sought to dismantle the system of segregation and discrimination that had oppressed African Americans for centuries.

The movement was met with fierce resistance. Activists faced arrest, beatings, and even assassination as they fought for their rights. The terror they confronted was not just physical violence, but the entrenched racism that permeated American society. The fear of lynching, police brutality, and the Ku Klux Klan's terror tactics were real and present dangers.

Yet, the Civil Rights Movement was also a testament to the power of nonviolent resistance and the courage of those who refused to accept oppression. The struggle for freedom was not just a battle against legal and political systems but a fight to reclaim dignity, humanity, and justice.

The victories of the Civil Rights Movement—such as the Civil Rights Act of
1964 and the Voting Rights Act of 1965—marked significant milestones in the fight against oppression. But the legacy of this struggle is ongoing, as the fight for equality and justice continues in various forms to this day.

The Hidden Oppressions

41

Not all oppression is easy to see. Sometimes, it hides behind a surface of normal life, where systems of power and privilege create unfairness that is harder to spot but still harmful.

G

ender Oppression: The Silent Suffering

Gender oppression is one of the most pervasive forms of oppression, affecting millions of women and girls around
the world. It manifests in various ways—through domestic violence, discrimination in the workplace, denial of education, and cultural practices that devalue women's lives.

In many parts of the world, women live in fear of violence from their partners, families, or communities. The terror of gender-based violence is not just physical but psychological, as it reinforces a sense of powerlessness and fear. The stigma and shame associated with sexual violence further silence victims, trapping them in a cycle of fear and oppression.

The fight against gender oppression is ongoing, with movements such as #MeToo bringing global attention to the issue. Yet, the terror of living under a system that perpetuates inequality and violence against women remains a reality for many. The struggle for gender equality is a fight against a deep rooted system of oppression that requires not just legal and policy changes, but a transformation of societal attitudes and norms.

The Hope of Liberation

D

espite the terror of oppression, history is also filled with stories of liberation, where the oppressed have triumphed over their oppressors, reclaiming their rights and freedoms.

T

he Fall of the Berlin Wall: A Symbol of Freedom

The fall of the Berlin Wall in 1989 is one of the most powerful symbols of liberation in modern history. For nearly three decades,
the Wall had divided East and West Berlin, representing the broader division of Europe during the Cold War. The Wall was a physical and psychological barrier that separated families, restricted movement, and embodied the oppressive nature of the East German regime.

The peaceful protests that led to the Wall's fall were a testament to the power of the human spirit in the face of oppression. The images of East and West Berliners tearing down the Wall, celebrating their newfound freedom, resonated around the world. The fall of the Berlin Wall marked the beginning of the end for the oppressive regimes of Eastern Europe and symbolized the triumph of freedom over tyranny.

The hope of liberation is a powerful force that can overcome even the most entrenched systems of oppression. It is a reminder that, no matter how strong the oppressor, the desire for freedom and justice cannot be extinguished.

Conclusion: The Resilience of the Human Spirit

O

ppression is a source of profound terror, but it is also a force that has shaped some of the most significant struggles for justice and freedom in human history. The fear that oppression instills in its victims is real and devastating, but it also drives the oppressed to fight back, to resist, and to reclaim their humanity.

The resilience of the human spirit in the face of oppression is a testament to the enduring hope for a better world. Throughout history, those who have suffered under oppressive regimes, systems, and ideologies have found ways to resist, to survive, and to overcome. The terror of oppression may be powerful, but the desire for freedom, dignity, and justice is ultimately stronger.

Chapter 4: The Terror of Environmental Collapse

The Fragility of Nature

Environmental collapse is a terror that transcends borders, affecting every corner of the planet and every living being on it. Unlike other forms of terror, which may be localized or temporary, environmental collapse represents a global threat, one that endangers the very survival of humanity. The fear of losing the natural world—the forests, oceans, rivers, and wildlife that sustain life—is a fear that grips our collective consciousness, as we witness the gradual unraveling of ecosystems upon which we all depend.

The Amazon Rainforest: The Lungs of the Earth in Peril

The Amazon Rainforest, often referred to as the "lungs of the Earth," is one of the most critical ecosystems on the planet. It plays a vital role in regulating the global climate, absorbing vast amounts of carbon dioxide and producing oxygen. However, this ancient and biodiverse forest is under siege from deforestation, illegal logging, mining, and agricultural expansion.

The terror of the Amazon's destruction is not just in the immediate loss of trees or wildlife, but in the long-term consequences for the global climate. The fear is that the Amazon may reach a tipping point, where the damage becomes irreversible, leading to its transformation from a carbon sink into a carbon source. This could accelerate global warming, leading to more extreme weather events, rising sea levels, and widespread ecological collapse.

F

or the indigenous peoples who call the Amazon home, the terror is deeply personal. The destruction of the forest means the loss of their land, culture, and way of life. The fear of being displaced, of losing their ancestral home to the relentless march of industrialization, is a daily reality. The terror of environmental collapse in the Amazon is a reminder that the destruction of nature is also the destruction of human lives and communities.

The Scourge of Pollution

P

ollution is a pervasive threat that affects air, water, and soil, endangering human health and the environment. The terror of pollution is the fear of living in a world where the very elements that sustain life—air, water, and food—become sources of harm.

Air Pollution: The Invisible Killer

Air pollution is one of the most significant environmental health risks, responsible for millions of premature deaths each year. The sources of air pollution are varied—burning fossil fuels, industrial emissions, vehicle exhaust, and agricultural activities—all contributing to the release of harmful pollutants like particulate matter, nitrogen oxides, and sulfur dioxide into the atmosphere.

The terror of air pollution is in its invisibility. Unlike other environmental threats, air pollution is often not seen but is always present, infiltrating homes, schools, and workplaces. The fear is not just of the immediate health effects, such as respiratory and cardiovascular diseases, but of the long-term consequences, including cancer, neurological damage, and reduced life expectancy.

The terror of living in a world where the air is toxic is a constant anxiety for many, particularly in densely populated urban areas where pollution levels are highest. The fear of not being able to protect oneself or one's family from this invisible threat adds to the psychological burden, creating a pervasive sense of helplessness.

The Biodiversity

Crisis

B

iodiversity, the variety of life on Earth, is in rapid decline, with species going extinct at an alarming rate. This loss of biodiversity is not just an environmental issue but a profound threat to human survival.

T

he Sixth Mass Extinction: A Planet in Peril

Scientists warn that we are currently living through the sixth mass extinction, driven by human activities such as habitat destruction,
overexploitation, pollution, and climate change. Unlike previous mass extinctions, which were caused by natural events like asteroid impacts or volcano eruptions, this one is the result of human actions.

The terror of biodiversity loss is the fear of living in a world devoid of the richness and beauty of life. The extinction of species is not just a loss for nature but a loss for humanity, as we depend on biodiversity for food, medicine, clean air and water, and countless other ecosystem services.

The fear is also existential—the knowledge that by driving other species to extinction, we may be endangering our own future. The loss of pollinators like bees threatens global food production, while the destruction of forests and wetlands increases the risk of natural disasters and pandemics. The terror of environmental collapse in the form of biodiversity loss is a reminder that we are part of the web of life, and when that web unravels, so too does the fabric of human civilization.

The Climate

Crisis

C limate change is perhaps the most all-encompassing threat of environmental collapse, affecting every aspect of life on Earth. The terror of climate change is the fear of an uncertain and increasingly
hostile future.

E

xtreme Weather: Nature's Fury Unleashed

As the planet warms, we are witnessing an increase in the frequency and intensity of extreme weather events—hurricanes, floods, droughts, wildfires, and heatwaves. These events are not just natural disasters but manifestations of a changing climate, driven by human activities such as burning fossil fuels and deforestation.

The terror of extreme weather is the fear of being caught in a disaster that you cannot control or escape. The unpredictability of these events adds to the anxiety, as communities struggle to prepare for and respond to increasingly severe and frequent storms, floods, and fires. The fear is also economic, as extreme weather causes billions of dollars in damage each year, destroying homes, infrastructure, and livelihoods.

The terror of climate change is also psychological—the fear of a future where the planet becomes increasingly uninhabitable, where droughts lead to food shortages, floods displace millions of people, and rising temperatures make entire regions unlivable. The fear of climate change is not just the fear of natural disasters but the fear of a world where life as we know it may no longer be possible.

The Struggle for Survival

I

n the face of environmental collapse, the struggle for survival becomes a daily reality for many communities around the world. The terror of environmental degradation is a reminder that humanity's relationship with nature is fragile and that our actions have profound consequences for the planet's future.

The Pacific Islands: A People at the Brink

T

he Pacific Islands are among the most vulnerable regions to the impacts of climate change. Rising sea levels, caused by the melting of polar ice and the thermal expansion of seawater, are threatening to submerge entire islands, displacing communities and wiping out cultures that have existed for millennia.

The terror for the people of the Pacific Islands is the fear of losing their homeland, their identity, and their way of life. The fear is not just of the physical loss of land but of the cultural and spiritual connection to that land, which is integral to their sense of self and community. The prospect of becoming climate refugees, forced to leave their ancestral homes and resettle in foreign lands, is a terrifying and deeply unsettling reality.

The struggle for survival in the face of environmental collapse is a fight to protect not just land and resources but the very essence of what it means to be human. It is a battle against a force that seems unstoppable, but also a testament to the resilience and determination of those who refuse to give up.

Chapter 5: The Terror of Disease

The Fear of the Unknown

I

n South Africa, the arrival of a new illness brings a strong sense of fear. For generations, people have lived off the land, using traditional knowledge to treat common illnesses. But when a new disease appears,
one they've never seen before, the fear of the unknown spreads even faster than the illness itself.

E

bola: A Community Paralyzed by Fear

The Ebola outbreak that swept through West Africa in 2014 is a stark example of the terror of disease. It began with a single case in
a small village in Guinea, but within months, it had spread across borders, devastating communities in Liberia, Sierra Leone, and beyond. The fear that accompanied the outbreak was

overwhelming. Families were torn apart as loved ones were taken to isolation units, often never to be seen again. Misinformation and mistrust fueled panic, leading some to flee from health workers rather than seek help.

For those living in affected areas, every cough, every fever, became a source of anxiety. The sight of protective suits, once a symbol of safety, became a reminder of the invisible enemy lurking among them. The terror of disease is not just the fear of falling ill; it is the fear of the unknown, of an enemy that cannot be seen, predicted, or easily defeated.

The fear extended beyond those directly affected by the outbreak. Internationally, Ebola sparked panic, with people around the world worrying about the possibility of the disease reaching their own communities. The uncertainty about how the virus spread, the lack of a cure, and the images of suffering broadcast across the globe created a climate of fear that was difficult to contain.

The Inescapable Reach of Pandemics

W

hile Ebola was a localized outbreak, the terror of disease can reach far beyond the borders of any one country. In our interconnected world, a disease that emerges in one part of
the globe can quickly become a global threat, as seen with the COVID-19 pandemic.

COVID-19: A World Brought to Its Knees

The COVID-19 pandemic, which began in late 2019, demonstrated the terrifying speed at which a disease can spread in a globalized world. What started as a mysterious illness in a Chinese city soon escalated into a worldwide crisis, affecting every corner of the globe.

The fear of COVID-19 was multifaceted. Initially, it was the fear of the unknown—what is this virus, and how dangerous is it? As the virus spread, the fear evolved into anxiety over the health of loved ones, the strain on healthcare systems, and the economic fallout of lockdowns and restrictions.

For many, the terror of disease during the pandemic was amplified by isolation. As governments implemented social distancing measures to curb the spread of the virus, people were cut off from friends, family, and community support. The isolation created a mental health crisis, with skyrocketing rates of anxiety, depression, and loneliness. The fear of contracting the virus was compounded by the fear of enduring the pandemic alone.

T

he Long Shadow of Long COVID

Even as vaccines and treatments became available, the terror of COVID-19 did not fully dissipate. The emergence of "Long COVID"—a condition where symptoms persist for months, even years, after the initial infection—added a new layer of fear. For those affected, the disease became a long-term battle, with no clear end in sight. The uncertainty of
whether or when they might fully recover added to the psychological toll, making the terror of disease an enduring presence in their lives.

The Economic Devastation of Disease

T

he terror of disease extends beyond the immediate health impacts to the broader social and economic consequences. Pandemics and epidemics can cripple economies, deepen inequalities, and push
already vulnerable populations to the brink.

H
IV/AIDS: A Global Epidemic

The HIV/AIDS epidemic, which began in the 1980s, is one of the most devastating examples of the far-reaching impact of disease. Initially, the virus spread largely unnoticed, confined to specific communities. But as it became clear that HIV/AIDS was not limited by geography, race, or sexual orientation, the fear it engendered grew.

In many parts of Africa, the impact of HIV/AIDS has been catastrophic. The disease decimated entire communities, leaving behind millions of orphans and overwhelming healthcare systems. The economic toll was equally severe. In countries where the majority of the workforce was affected, productivity plummeted, and poverty deepened. The fear of contracting HIV/AIDS led to stigma and discrimination, further isolating those already suffering.

For individuals, the diagnosis of HIV/AIDS was, for many years, a death sentence. The terror of the disease was not just in the physical suffering it caused, but in the social ostracization and the knowledge that there was no cure, no hope of recovery. The advent of antiretroviral therapy has transformed HIV/AIDS from a fatal disease to a manageable condition, but the terror it inspired in its early days is a reminder of the devastating power of disease.

The Social Stigma of Disease

D

isease often causes not just physical pain, but also social stigma. The fear of illness can cause people to push the sick away, making them outcasts and worsening their suffering.

Leprosy: The Ancient Fear

Leprosy, also known as Hansen's disease, is one of the oldest recorded diseases in human history. For millennia, those afflicted with leprosy were shunned, forced to live in isolation, and treated as outcasts. The terror of leprosy was not just the physical deformities it caused, but the social exclusion that came with it.

In many cultures, leprosy was seen as a punishment from the gods, a sign of moral failing or divine wrath. This belief led to the harsh treatment of those with the disease, who were often banished from their communities and forced to live in leper colonies. The fear of leprosy was so great that even today, despite the fact that it is curable, the stigma persists in some parts of the world.

The story of leprosy is a reminder of how the fear of disease can lead to the dehumanization of those who suffer from it. It shows how terror can be not just a personal experience, but a collective one, rooted in cultural beliefs and social practices that persist long after the disease itself is no longer a major threat.

The Hope of Medical Advances

Despite the terror of disease, there is also hope. Advances in medicine and public health have made it possible to prevent, treat, and even eradicate many diseases that once struck fear into the hearts of people around the world.

T

he Victory Over Smallpox

One of the greatest triumphs in the fight against disease is the eradication of smallpox. For centuries, smallpox was one of the most feared diseases, responsible for millions of deaths worldwide. The virus caused severe illness, characterized by a painful rash, high fever, and often death. Even those who survived were left with permanent scars.

The terror of smallpox was such that it led to the development of one of the earliest vaccines, created by Edward Jenner in the late 18th century. Over the next two centuries, concerted efforts to vaccinate populations around the world led to the eventual eradication of smallpox in 1980, a milestone in public health history.

The story of smallpox eradication is a testament to the power of science and international cooperation in overcoming the terror of disease. It shows that, with the right tools and the collective will, even the most feared diseases can be defeated.

The Ongoing Battle Against Emerging Diseases

While the eradication of smallpox is a triumph, the fight against disease is far from over. New diseases continue to emerge, and the threat of pandemics remains. The ongoing battle against diseases like malaria, tuberculosis, and HIV/AIDS, as well as the challenge of preparing for future pandemics, requires constant vigilance and innovation.

The development of new vaccines, treatments, and public health strategies offers hope that we can continue to mitigate the terror of disease. But it also requires a commitment to equity, ensuring that all people, regardless of where they live or how much they earn, have access to the care they need.

Conclusion: The Duality of Disease

T

he terror of disease is a dual force. On one hand, it represents the fear of the unknown, the dread of suffering, and the anxiety of losing control over one's body and life. On the other hand, it is a force that has driven some of humanity's greatest achievements in science and medicine.

Throughout history, the fear of disease has prompted innovation, solidarity, and resilience. It has led to the development of vaccines, the improvement of sanitation, and the establishment of healthcare systems that save millions of lives every year. Yet, the terror remains, as new diseases emerge and old ones resurface.

The fight against disease is a reminder of both the fragility and the strength of the human condition. It is a battle that we must continue to wage, not just with science, but with compassion, equity, and a commitment to the well-being of all people.

Chapter 6: The Terror of Isolation

The Descent into Solitude

Isolation is a profound and often underestimated form of terror. It manifests as both physical and emotional separation from others, leading to a sense of abandonment and disconnection. The fear of isolation is rooted in our fundamental need for social connection and the existential dread that accompanies being cut off from the world.

he Loneliness of Remote Communities

In the remote reaches of the world, isolation is a daily reality for many. Communities situated in harsh and inaccessible environments, such as Arctic villages, deep jungle tribes, or isolated island settlements, often experience a form of isolation that goes beyond physical distance.

A

rctic Villages: The Perils of Extreme Isolation

In Arctic villages like Barrow, Alaska, or Longyearbyen, Norway, the isolation is both geographical and temporal. These communities face extreme weather conditions and prolonged periods of darkness during winter months. The harsh environment is compounded by the difficulty of accessing outside resources and support. The terror here is the combination of physical isolation from the rest of the world and the psychological toll of living in an environment that seems inhospitable.

For residents of these Arctic villages, isolation manifests as a constant struggle against both nature and loneliness. The fear of being cut off from medical help, supplies, or even social contact during extreme weather conditions heightens the sense of vulnerability. The psychological impact of prolonged isolation, where the sun may not rise for months, can lead to depression, anxiety, and a profound sense of desolation.

The Modern Epidemic of Loneliness

I

n an age of unprecedented connectivity through technology, loneliness and isolation are paradoxically on the rise. Despite being more
"connected" than ever, many people experience profound feelings of loneliness and social disconnection.

U

rban Isolation: The Paradox of Connectedness

In bustling cities like New York, Tokyo, or London, where people are surrounded by millions of others, isolation can still be a pervasive issue. The phenomenon of urban isolation is characterized by a sense of loneliness amidst a sea of people. The anonymity and transience of city life can lead to a lack of meaningful connections and support networks.

The terror of urban isolation is the fear of being surrounded by people yet feeling utterly alone. The fast pace of city life, the focus on individual success, and the lack of communal spaces contribute to a sense of disconnection. The psychological effects of urban isolation can be severe, including depression, anxiety, and a heightened sense of alienation.

The Digital Dystopia

hile digital technology has the potential to connect people across the globe, it can also exacerbate feelings of isolation.

Social media and virtual interactions can create a veneer of connectivity while deepening the sense of loneliness and disconnection in real life.

V

irtual Realities and Real-Life Disconnection

The rise of social media platforms, online gaming, and virtual reality has transformed how we interact, but it has also led to a new form of isolation. People may spend hours interacting with avatars or digital representations of others, while their real-world relationships suffer from neglect. The terror here is the growing disparity between virtual connections and real-life interactions.

The curated nature of social media can also lead to feelings of inadequacy and loneliness, as individuals compare their own lives to the seemingly perfect lives of others. The sense of being excluded from meaningful social interactions can deepen the feeling of isolation, creating a cycle where digital engagement replaces genuine human contact.

The Isolation of Mental Illness

M

ental illness can also lead to profound isolation, as those affected may withdraw from social interactions due to stigma, fear, or a lack of understanding from others. The terror of mental illness-induced isolation is the fear of being cut off from support and understanding while grappling with one's own struggles.

Depression and Social Withdrawal

Depression is often accompanied by a sense of isolation and disconnection. Individuals suffering from depression may find it difficult to engage with others, leading to social withdrawal and a feeling of being alone in their struggles. The terror of this type of isolation is the compounded feeling of being both overwhelmed by personal suffering and abandoned by those who could provide support.

The stigma surrounding mental illness can further exacerbate isolation, as individuals may fear judgment or rejection if they seek help. The internal battle of managing mental health issues while dealing with external perceptions of weakness or failure can create a profound sense of isolation and loneliness.

The Fear of Social Exclusion

I

solation is not only a matter of physical or geographical distance but also of social exclusion. Being deliberately or inadvertently excluded from social groups, communities, or societal participation can create a
deep and lasting sense of isolation.

The Marginalized and Disenfranchised

Social exclusion can affect various groups, including marginalized communities, refugees, the elderly, or those with disabilities. The fear of being excluded from social participation and support networks is a constant reality for many. This type of isolation can result in a lack of access to resources, opportunities, and social engagement, deepening feelings of abandonment and worthlessness.

The terror of social exclusion is the fear of being invisible or irrelevant, of living on the fringes of society without a place or purpose. The psychological impact of exclusion can be severe, leading to depression, anxiety, and a loss of identity and self-worth.

The Existential

Terror

A t its core, the terror of isolation is existential. It touches on the fundamental human need for connection, purpose, and belonging.
 The fear of being truly alone in a vast, indifferent world can lead to profound existential dread.

T

he Void of Existence

The existential terror of isolation is the fear of being insignificant, of existing without meaning or connection. It is the dread of facing one's own mortality or the end of one's place in the world without the comfort of companionship or purpose.

This existential fear can drive individuals to seek connection, meaning, and community, even in the face of overwhelming odds. It is a reminder of the importance of human relationships and the need for empathy and understanding in combating the terror of isolation.

Conclusion: Bridging the Chasms

T

he terror of isolation is a multifaceted and deeply affecting experience, touching on physical, emotional, and existential dimensions. It is a reminder of our inherent need for connection and the profound effects that disconnection and solitude can have on individuals and societies.

To address the terror of isolation, it is essential to foster genuine human connections, build supportive communities, and address the underlying causes of social and emotional disconnection. By acknowledging and confronting the fear of isolation, we can work towards creating a world where people are not only physically connected but also emotionally and socially supported.

The struggle against isolation is a struggle for human connection, understanding, and empathy. It is a fight to ensure that no one is left alone in their terror, and that everyone has a place, purpose, and a sense of belonging.

Conclusion: Confronting the Terrors of Our World

The journey through the various forms of terror explored in this book reveals the profound and often hidden fears that shape our existence. From the environmental collapse threatening our planet to the pervasive isolation that cuts us off from one another, these terrors underscore the fragility of our world and the human condition.

Understanding the Shadows

Each chapter has illuminated a different facet of fear, whether it's the destruction of nature, the crisis of environmental degradation, or the existential dread of being alone. These terrors, while diverse in their manifestations, share a common thread: they all highlight our vulnerability and the intricate connections between our actions and their far-reaching consequences.

T

he Imperative of Action

Acknowledging these fears is the first step toward confronting them. Understanding the magnitude of environmental collapse, recognizing the impact of isolation, and addressing the various terrors that challenge our world, compel us to take action. It is not enough to simply be aware of these issues; we must actively engage in efforts to mitigate their effects and work towards solutions.

F

ostering Resilience and Connection

In facing these terrors, we must build resilience—both individually and collectively. This means fostering communities that support each other, advocating for environmental preservation, and addressing mental health challenges with compassion and understanding. By strengthening our connections with one another and with the natural world, we can confront these fears with solidarity and purpose.

E

mbracing Hope and Action

Despite the darkness that these terrors reveal, there is hope. The human capacity for empathy, creativity, and resilience offers a beacon of light in the face of overwhelming challenges. By uniting our efforts and nurturing our shared humanity, we can create a world where fear does not paralyze us but propels us towards positive change.

This book serves as a reminder that the terrors of our world, while daunting, are not insurmountable. Through awareness, action, and connection, we can confront these fears and work towards a future where we live in harmony with each other and the planet. The journey is ongoing, and it is up to each of us to play our part in shaping a world that reflects hope, resilience, and collective strength.

Thank you for joining me on this exploration of the terrors that shape our world. May it inspire us to face our fears with courage and determination, and to build a future where we overcome these challenges together.

www.ingramcontent.com/pod-product-compliance
Lightning Source LLC
Chambersburg PA
CBHW061514250726
48657CB00005B/1860